D1562745

THIS IS A BOOK ABOUT FIRE

Woodland

poems | *with music by*
KNOX GARDNER | AARON OTHEIM

ENTRE RÍOS BOOKS

WWW.ENTRERIOSBOOKS.COM

SEATTLE, WASHINGTON

WOODLAND

TEXT COPYRIGHT ©2019 KNOX GARDNER

MUSIC COPYRIGHT @2019 AARON OTHEIM

ISBN: 978-0-9600457-0-9 (PAPER)

COVER IMAGE. ©2017 CHRIS LIEDLE

EAGLE CREEK FIRE BURNING IN THE COLUMBIA RIVER GORGE ON SEPTEMBER 4, 2017

WWW.CHRISLIEDLEPHOTO.COM

INTERIOR PHOTOS BY LICENSE FROM STOCK.ADOBE.COM

FIRST EDITION / ERB 010

PRINTED IN THE UNITED STATES

DENDRO

The forest in the drawer
herbaceous con-
densation

knowing is chain well adjusted:
living reasons
the saw, reasons the
measure
of dissection & division.

Felled the tree,
green unwilding

untidy laminate
— pollen & seed —
manufactured

this boxed figuration.

the stripping fence
cedars, waxwings
in bough
gracious what streams
the dimmest sound
fairest
buffered sea oats & bluestem
but sloshes
with my ungainly hoof

when —

sintering & barbless
confinement beads the heart,
where —

night brings its buses, the emptying
its torn fabrics & limping

O hunger
this again alights

the chaining tree
how it beckons
destruction
angled
on the slope

the gable stud
bears the slant, sheathing
compacted — great
is the silence

where uncertain means
the sky

a world that

(spins

this cut weather of dry lumber
ferocious as ever

O the bed & buckskin
chitters the fog
that finds no height —

it rolls through the north coast
weary and homeless
tho picnic tables
& cardboard
& the foam that laps

Were you the extravagant match,
the field of slander sticks?

O tinder,
such staggered palmistry the way
one cups a flame
in the roaring wind.

The chimes unbalance
the filling sky, how it pelts us
with sorrows

so empty without
us — without our fanning worry.

I was that field when I heard
the striking.

And the wald & its bridge
— the unnearing music
its embers,

such wooden
horses & needling
gowns. I might take

the axe, the rake, the hoe.

I might stand back & watch
it burn.

The forest master twists,

the unmastered forest
its rev list.

SOME BURNING : 2017

JAN 02	CHILE	Fire Destroys Homes above Chilean Port City
JAN 12	INDONESIA	Choppers Sent to Fight Forest Fires in Riau
JAN 18	KENYA	Fire Breaks out Afresh in Aberdare National Forest
JAN 19	CHILE	Fires Threaten Vineyards in Colchagua Valley
JAN 22	AUSTRALIA	Firies Prepare for Long Night in Yuraygir NP
JAN 26	CHILE	Nine Dead in Chile's Forest Fires
JAN 26	INDIA	Wildfire Doused in Nagarahole Forest
JAN 29	PAKISTAN	Wildfire in Azad Kashmir Destroys Entire Market
FEB 02	SOUTH AFRICA	Wildfire Rages in the Hawequas Mountains
FEB 05	CHILE	Just 50 Forest Fires Now Burning Govt Says
FEB 06	INDIA	Fire in Sikkim's Fambong Lho Wildlife Sanctuary
FEB 07	CHINA	Wildfire Burns Forest in Ngaba's Dzoege
FEB 09	COLOMBIA	Authorities Fight Six Forest Fires
FEB 17	AUSTRALIA	Firefighters Injured in Fast-Moving Fire
FEB 17	NEW ZEALAND	More Than 1400 Fire Evacuees Able to Return
FEB 18	INDIA	Wildfire Devastates Mudumalai Tiger Reserve
FEB 19	UNITED STATES	Crews Contain Fire that Burned about 600 Acres
FEB 19	INDIA	Officials Struggle to Put out Fire at Bandipur Forest
FEB 22	CHILE	Wildfires Continue in Chile
FEB 22	INDIA	1000 Hectares of Trees Burnt at Seshachalam Forest
FEB 25	UNITED STATES	18 Fires Intentionally Set in North Carolina
FEB 27	INDIA	Madugani Forest Fire Wipes out Acres of Teak
MAR 01	INDIA	Kali Tiger Reserve Bears Brunt of Fire
MAR 05	UNITED STATES	Forest Fires Break out in Eastern Kentucky
MAR 06	UNITED STATES	1500-Acre Fire Burning in Picayune Strand, Florida
MAR 06	INDIA	Fire Destroys 10,000 Acres of Forest in Mudigere
MAR 07	UNITED STATES	Fire Started in Amarillo, 90% Contained
MAR 08	UNITED STATES	Wildfires Burn 1 Million Acres, Taking 7 Lives
MAR 08	UNITED STATES	Brush Fire Shuts Down Part of Alligator Alley
MAR 09	BHUTAN	200 Acres of Forest Destroyed by Fire at Yangnyer
MAR 11	KENYA	Fire Destroys 50 Hectares of Menengai Forest

MAR 12	CHILE	Thousands Flee Central Chile Forest Fire
MAR 13	INDIA	Fire at Baghdara Destroys the Nature Park
MAR 14	UNITED KINGDOM	Evacuations as Wildfire Blazes in Moray Grassland
MAR 15	KENYA	Fires Consume Forests in Nyandarua, Nakuru
MAR 19	INDIA	Firefighters, Locals Fight Forest Fire in Uri Village
MAR 20	UNITED STATES	Evacuees Allowed Back near Colorado College Town
MAR 23	UNITED STATES	Fire Started by Book Burning Destroys 10 Homes
MAR 24	INDIA	In 2 Days 542 Forest Fires in Telangana
MAR 24	UNITED STATES	Fire Burns 60,000 Acres in Roberts County, Texas
MAR 26	IRELAND	Fires Roar across Ireland during Sunny Weekend
MAR 26	UNITED STATES	1000 People Evacuated after Colorado Wildfire
MAR 29	INDIA	IAF Chopper Helps Douse Forest Blaze in Udaipur
APR 02	UNITED KINGDOM	20 Firefighters Battle Wildfire in the Highlands
APR 05	CHINA	4 Firefighters Killed in North China Forest Fire
APR 05	INDIA	Fires Break Out in Corbett Tiger Reserve
APR 07	UNITED STATES	Wildfire Burning Northeast of Disney World
APR 10	UNITED STATES	Fire in Virginia Believed to Be Arson
APR 12	UNITED STATES	Residents Warned in Case Fires Prompt Evacuations
APR 12	UNITED KINGDOM	Wildfire Units Called to Massive Fire at Ranges
APR 17	INDIA	Forest Fire in Mount Abu Rages On
APR 22	VIETNAM	Fire Destroys 36 Hectares ff Cajuput Forest
APR 23	UNITED STATES	Arizona Fire Grows, Is Human-Caused
MAY 01	CHINA	Fire Engulfs Primeval Forest in North China
MAY 02	CHINA	Fire in Inner Mongolia Spreads to 10,000 Hectares
MAY 08	UNITED STATES	Fire In Gila National Forest Grows
MAY 10	IRELAND	Third of Ireland's Largest Forest Is Destroyed
MAY 14	GREECE	1 Dead, 2 Injured as Fire Scorches near Athens
MAY 15	UNITED STATES	Evacuation Order Lifted near Georgia Wildfire
MAY 15	UNITED STATES	Wildfire Burns 300+ Acres in Northern Minnesota
MAY 16	UNITED STATES	Puma Fire West of Colorado Springs Doubles
MAY 17	CHINA	Forest Fire Rages in North China

MAY 19	INDONESIA	Forest Fires Hit Sumatra Again, Causing Smog
MAY 22	UNITED STATES	Wildfire in California under Criminal Investigation
MAY 24	CANADA	Wildfire Burning Out of Control near Mt. Robson
MAY 24	UNITED STATES	Wildfire Forces Evacuations North of Leavenworth
JUN 12	CANADA	Crews Fighting Fire near Johnson's Crossing, Yukon
JUN 18	PORTUGAL	At Least 61 Killed, Many in Cars Overrun by Blaze
JUN 20	UNITED STATES	Wildfire Grows Amid Sweltering California Heat Wave
JUN 30	TURKEY	Major Fire Spreads across Alanya
JUL 02	UNITED STATES	Hwy 143 Opens up as Crews Report 65% Containment
JUL 03	PORTUGAL	Ten People Injured in New Portugal Forest Fires
JUL 04	UNITED STATES	Wildfire Forces Evacuations in Wyoming
JUL 04	UNITED STATES	Arizona's Frye Fire Balloons to 46,760 Acres
JUL 05	UNITED STATES	Fire Forces Evacuations near Colorado Ski Resort
JUL 05	CANADA	Business Destroyed, Homes Damaged by Wildfire
JUL 08	CANADA	Princeton Fire Holds at 1500 Hectares
JUL 08	CHINA	Fire Rages in North China Forest
JUL 10	UNITED STATES	5000 Firefighters Battling 14 Large Wildfires in CA
JUL 10	CANADA	BCils Burning, 14,000 People Displaced
JUL 12	ITALY	1000 Tourists Evacuated from Sicily Due to Wildfire
JUL 15	SPAIN	Fire Close to Badajoz as Heat Wave Continues
JUL 16	CANADA	Around 37,000 Residents Forced to Leave Their Homes
JUL 18	FRANCE	France Fights Forest Fires near Nice and Corsica
JUL 18	PORTUGAL	Portugal Starting to Bring Fires Under Control
JUL 18	MONTENEGRO	Fire in Croatia, Montenegro Asks for Help
JUL 19	UNITED STATES	Wildfire Rages in Western US, Thousands Evacuated
JUL 20	ISRAEL	Homes Evacuated as Forest Fire nears Jerusalem
JUL 20	CANADA	Evacuations after Wildfire on Outskirts of Penticton
JUL 21	ITALY	Fires Stretching Capacity of Fire Department
JUL 26	GREECE	Firefighters Battling 19 Wildfires across Greece
JUL 26	FRANCE	Fires Prompt 10,000 Evacuations on French Riviera
JUL 27	PORTUGAL	Strong Winds, Dry Forests Fuel Portugal Fires

JUL 27	**FRANCE**	Wildfires Keep Breaking out in France & Portugal
JUL 30	**UNITED STATES**	Firefighters Investigate 7 Fires in Missouri
JUL 31	**CANADA**	Homes Remain Evacuated after Fire in New Brunswick
JUL 31	**TUNISIA**	Authorities Evacuating Citizens after Outbreak of Fires
AUG 01	**GREECE**	Overnight Battle with the Flames South of Athens
AUG 01	**UNITED STATES**	Hwy 178 Still Closed as Fire Grows
AUG 03	**GREECE**	Firefighters Battle Blaze in the Peloponnese
AUG 05	**GREECE**	Wildfire Rages on Greek Island of Kythera
AUG 07	**UNITED STATES**	National Guard to Fight Fire in Montana
AUG 08	**UNITED STATES**	Lightning Sparks Fires in Umpqua National Forest
AUG 10	**TURKEY**	Arson Suspected in Simultaneous Forest Fires
AUG 11	**GREECE**	Firefighters Battle 54 Blazes across Greece
AUG 11	**ALBANIA**	Wildfires Rage across Albania
AUG 15	**PORTUGAL**	3000 Firefighters Combat Raging Wildfire
AUG 16	**GREECE**	Greece Declares State of Emergency
AUG 19	**GREENLAND**	Massive Peat Fire Burns over Two Weeks
AUG 20	**PORTUGAL**	Copter Combating Fire Crashes in Portugal
AUG 21	**CROTIA**	Dozens of Fires along Adriatic Coast
AUG 22	**CANADA**	Fire Forces Evacuation of Poplar River
AUG 23	**CROATIA**	Several Fires Raging on Croatia's Adriatic Coast
AUG 25	**GEORGIA**	Belarusian Helicopter Drops Water on Fire
AUG 26	**UNITED STATES**	Wildfires Rage throughout Southwest Oregon
AUG 26	**UNITED STATES**	Fast-Growing Blaze Threatens Ranches in Montana
SEP 03	**UNITED STATES**	Gaining against Largest Blaze in Los Angeles History
SEP 04	**UNITED STATES**	Dozens Of Fires in Oregon Casting Pall Of Smoke
SEP 06	**UNITED STATES**	Fire Still Burning in the Gorge, Multnomah Falls Spared
SEP 06	**TURKEY**	Locals Evacuated as Fire Hits Western Turkey
SEP 13	**UNITED STATES**	Southeastern Arizona Fire Season Goes Wild
SEP 13	**UNITED STATES**	Large Fires Burning across Sierra Nevada
SEP 13	**CANADA**	Wildfire Shuts down Natural Gas Production
SEP 21	**SPAIN**	Wall of Flames Force Hundreds to Flee Homes

SEP 23	**UNITED STATES**	Wildfire Burning near Vacaville Destroys 3 Homes
OCT 02	**CANADA**	Forest Fire Breaks out across Okanagan Lake
OCT 03	**BANGLADESH**	Forest Fire Feared in Sundarbans
OCT 05	**UNITED STATES**	NH Fire Grows in Size Causing Utter Destruction
OCT 07	**PORTUGAL**	Fire Devil Captured on Camera during Wildfires
OCT 09	**AUSTRALIA**	Bushfire Burning near Karratha
OCT 11	**UNITED STATES**	Wildfires Ravage California, at Least 21 Killed
OCT 15	**SPAIN**	Raging Wildfires Kill 2 , Trigger Panic & Evacuations
OCT 16	**PORTUGAL**	27 Dead, 51 Injured as Portugal Suffers 500 Fires
OCT 16	**SPAIN**	Terrorist Arsonists Are Blamed for Wildfires
OCT 18	**UNITED STATES**	Lightning Fires Continue to Burn
OCT 22	**FRANCE**	Corsica Wildfire Ravages 2000 Hectares of Forest
OCT 23	**UNITED STATES**	Firefighters Still Battling 10 Wildfires in California
OCT 26	**ISRAEL**	Fire Raging in Sataf National Forest
OCT 30	**ITALY**	Fires Scorch Northern Italy, Evacuation of Hundreds
NOV 15	**INDIA**	Raging Fire Destroys Trees, Medicinal Herbs in Kupwara
NOV 29	**UNITED STATES**	Two Arkansas Forest Fires Nearly in Hand
DEC 04	**UNITED STATES**	Wildfire Threatens Hundreds of Homes North of LA
DEC 06:	**UNITED STATES**	27,000 Evacuated in California Due to Forest Fires
DEC 06:	**INDIA**	Forest Fire Erupts Along LoC in Poonch
DEC 08	**UNITED STATES**	Wildfire Destroys Mobile Homes in CA Retirement Park
DEC 10	**UNITED STATES**	CA Wildfire Rages Toward Scenic Coastal Communities
DEC 11	**UNITED STATES**	Fire Explodes to 230,500 Acres, Evacuations Ordered
DEC 13	**BHUTAN**	Forest Fire Rages in Chaapchha Gewog
DEC 14	**UNITED STATES**	Colossal California Fire—4th Largest in State History
DEC 15	**UNITED STATES**	Huge California Wildfire Continues to Grow
DEC 18	**UNITED STATES**	Burning in Pisgah National Forest under Investigation
DEC 18	**UNITED STATES**	Thomas Fire Raging, Still Threatening Santa Barbara
DEC 21	**UNITED STATES**	Custer State Park, South Dakota Wildfire Contained
DEC 24	**UNITED STATES**	Thomas Fire Is 88 Percent Contained
DEC 27	**SPAIN**	Wildfire Forces Evacuations in Spanish Tourist Resort

WOODLAND

I

To a Wild Rose

Edward Mac Dowell
Op. 51

With simple tenderness.

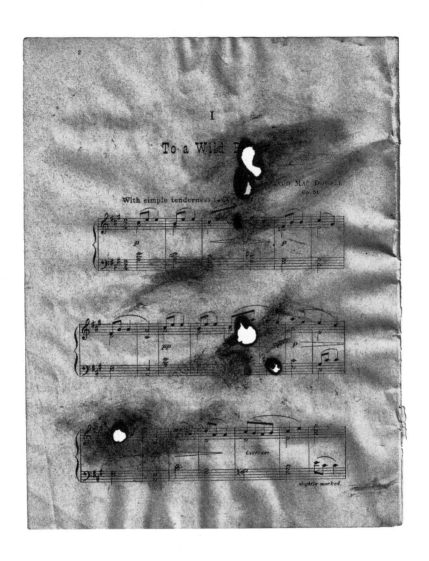

ONE: A WILD TENDER

wild roses stern-
hipped — fieldfare

field-edged &
clamber

O pinch scarlet, this giving

let ((pleasing

immemorial tho what
I said was just

this once always shifted
always

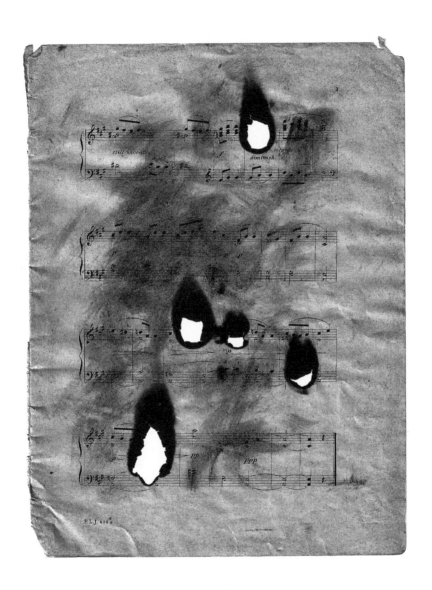

& so loved

the mortar
of this world (flakes)

to be unheld
— accursed

& lo
& lo

teeters (the cart)

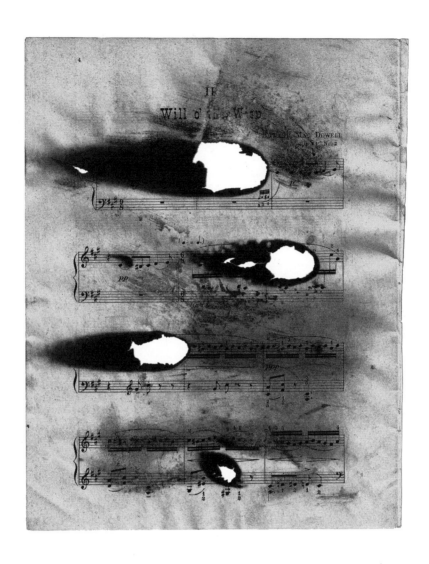

TWO: A SWIFT WILLING LIGHT

the pulp mountain
aside, the little machines
churn what is

iced, what is
stilling

& iced & slurried

the hawser drags the fire
behind

black waves & a carbon hook

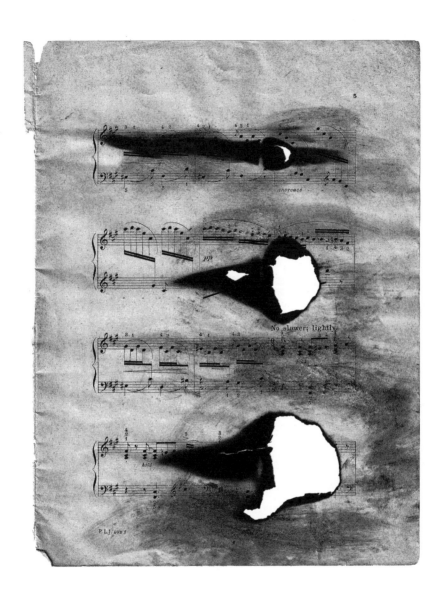

swift tho
Greenland's lit peat
&

our gates left open
the machines, less
tho black tho coal

[time]

near &

near
the ice fields
stairwell made of waves

weres
no

there is no nights
left, no

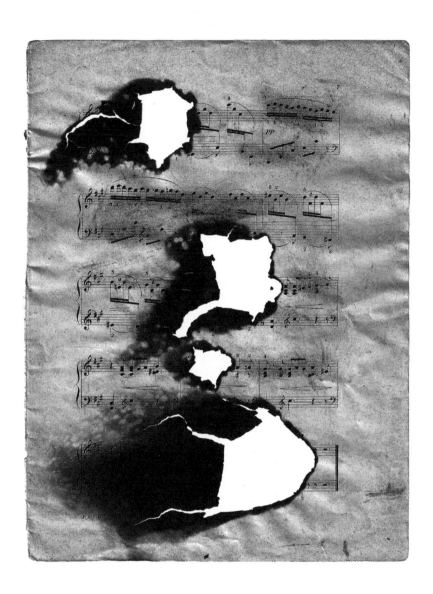

I watch them eat food, video
after video
of them eating, the

night dome is broken —
the shipping
containers, the unfrozen sea

I am ready

no moons
or that which it holds

THREE: THE TRY

the door is always
locked, the cut over

land —

slabbed houses put
against freeways

plank
after plank

poplars rearrange
themselves &
coyotes

FOUR: AUTUMN ALMOST

burnish summer
& tho

[a sadness]

wind inconstant, wind
as my own
little machines eat
everything the machines

(our wolves

barred & undernear, panting

those little
hungers, pitching the joints

pitching

fitfull & shakes,
sparrows
flirt
on as turbines dig

a quarry
once a GREAT FLOOD

                — smoke chips
coyote-willow
&

O how blades heave the rock

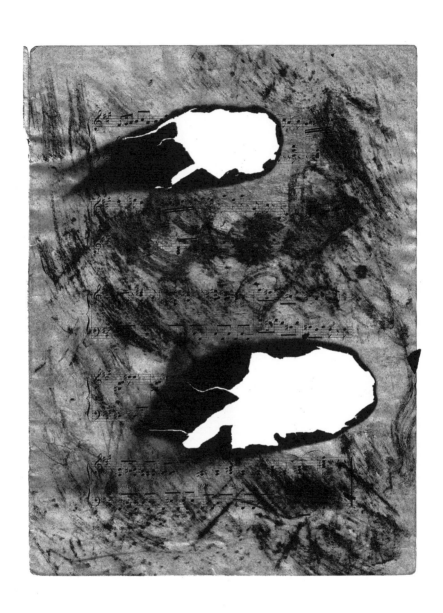

&
the grunting
& a hurry

[the wait   ]

fattening up what
machines shire the fur
of long winter
— always ahead somewhere

our quarry fills
our answers but

lo
where they fall

FIVE: STERN & MOURN

the belly of the whale
is mournful

[night   ]

O pitch burr,
O little thorns

O soot on the needles & sashes

the shearling
sea, fits

& starts any remonstrance

tho
a filthy memory

unknotting — reticence
& the off-season

(abashing
what was green, then

as always, song

SIX: TO A SWAYING

clasped the stays
movement of stars
dividing the —

the glassine
((shelter

soundless
& lo

upon
the awning   (

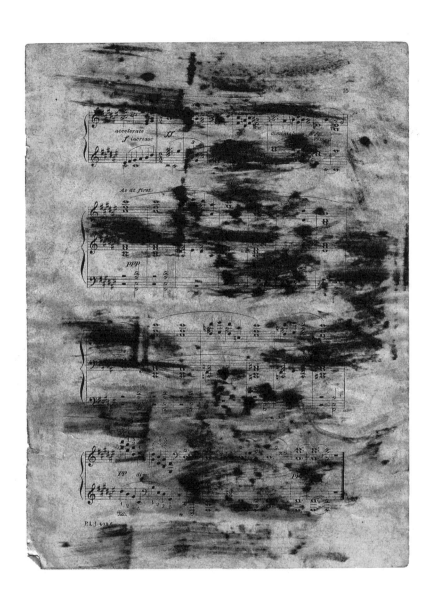

what night fears
gimbal — the slattering

wind
it scratches the ambulant
sky, slate tern wing
(what

a terror, a revulsion

that all of that
canopy gives

fire

SEVEN: WITH DRAGGING

drawing oft
& to light what remains
under-
ground

the barons, tell

& collapsible
O steady

O steady

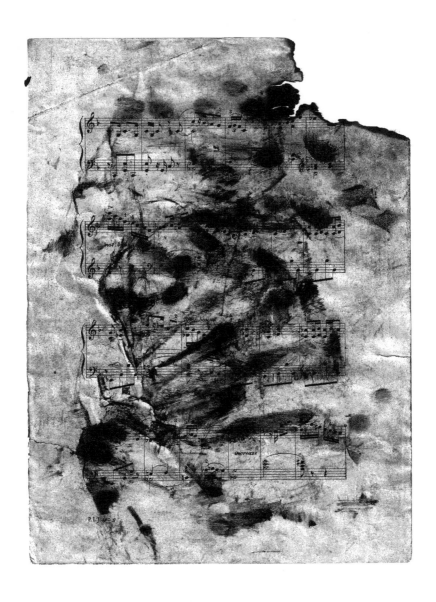

the agencies their
grubby hands — the little
machines copper-stripped
after-
market, even

(agencies

caught, un-
locked unawares

the machines, a crimping

so *yes*,
dissolution
& all the wires
& all the stone

(ALMIGHTY
the pulver lime, struck

match & Christ
the sky

(

EIGHT: DESERTED FARM

the liking box, felt
lin helder —
((inner

life keyed, targeted
& yes

approached
so softly, softly

[a shuffling]

a hand on the table
brace against the wall

— see how the match
trundles the straw

to quicken the barn
tho neither
quiet
nor soft

that's me
hard-heeled

&
looking you straight on

NINE: OFTEN A MEADOW

for Melinda Mueller

reclamation, spades
in marshes

willowed *what hunger*
at evenfall, swallows

these incessant —

(switches

some weaning bats, smudging

night

                        but
           the draindown —
           shinned & ditched
           (pause, a pleasure

           & catchwater

           so what
           then dries

           to green
           boundaries

           lo the fence
           how the wind whistles
           its afternoon

& the umbral fox?

in that redaction
of pasture, the queen's lace
ever bounds

through our singe
& sloughing

(

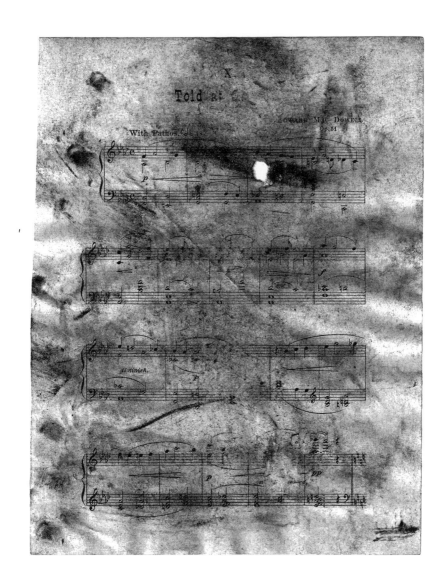

TEN: TOLD, OR A FINAL SETTING

Simon on the spar
skyline, main-
line & ye gathered

little shingles, little
shivs, how fragile

skid row, how slight
the bark it splinters

& there at remove
Simon pulleys &
the factory of the world

enacts its pressure
& spring

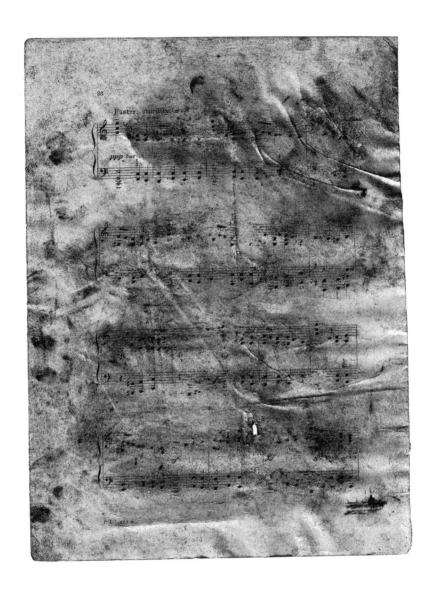

it's not the casting, Simon
it's who we are

loose
(& with matches

there's the heatstroke, there's
the bombs again

a bite of haze, there's the
sunburn, a fire squall

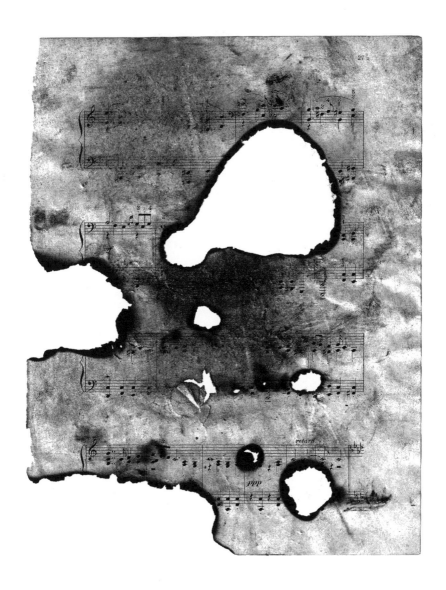

let me say we are too close

how swept the hem
it clangers its dust —

the small plates, the tilt door
& furor

(no the thread's on the cuff

the street swells the
people stoop
along
along

downwarfed, what is
the unsettling? this that

is scoured,
the roughed waterfront —
dark log-rafts through night

HARD CLIMATE NEVER

enter the woodman:

enter suppression:
brings the Nation its salvage
board, offerings
clean & willed — how stiffening
these

fallows upended, root
weary

this is the Nation, hood-
eyed & yes
                    wearied

(memory
tho degraded
so
& blazing
such such blazing

the crown alight, how
it jumps & pegs
how it rears against the sky —

it roars two mouths
bladed, of

prophets but no

(censure

the jumping the jumping
a bearing
limb that loses

green & crossings

the factory
of the world corners
the pulp market
                    "keeps the bright lights"

O but the whistling, the huffing
what it takes & tries

the Chinese labor ready
thumbing their coffin apartments

(joy

a potted camellia its brown
flowers scattered on tile

the eating in this
world never

. stop
the winning box
gears everything
levers
outstretched, the whirring
lover & spruce
rise up the mountain
contorted
for cooling
air —

the purple deer
barrels
unseemly
into the blackened log

standing only moments
before slacking thirst
& if unsteady the need still drives
but then you
stumble into the scene

& the deer, instinctively,
as always,
bolts to its overdue
death

swift the sapwood,
how it boils
        how saws
        glint & oil

what screams, when the sky
itself collapses
when slips the bank in-
to the creek

(there —

never one end begets
only one

never

the Nation of merit
handholds a pit —

peers toward its own
aversion & stilts

Noah built the Ark
the rains come & go

& what can't be said
is the waves hear nothing

the car burnt out —
the angry scaffold

& tho
higher higher the scales
(

say: *and the flames rose round us*

forlorn,

O God

VARIORUM
"To Never See You Again Fills Me with Great Sadness."

in the distance someone is mowing
the forest or powering lights

[the world]

an encroaching drone
unspooling a ribbon of air

no tender
no hold

the tents of the Nation
sun & flap,

cardboard, gleanings
we watch them
rush the boats…we see the stave
of forest left behind

we watch them through
slaggish heaps
…
we watch them
& the day keens its blade

such is
as the agency, such as the machines
we watch we watch we watch we
watch them raise their hands
we watch them

& the company takes what

Who, in the dark, has cast the harbor-chain?

not the binding cord, not
the anger

the wind itself mills
the drying flanks, the telling

(fuel

not the beetles gnawing,
the pitch tubes & duff

O heave the chain —
the telling un-
does again
&

[the forest]

[the forest]

[the forest]

THE ROOF IS ON FIRE

THE ROOF, THE ROOF, THE ROOF IS ON FIRE
(WE DON'T NEED NO WATER, LET THE MOTHERFUCKER BURN)
(BURN, MOTHERFUCKER, BURN)

— ROCK MASTER SCOTT AND THE DYNAMIC THREE, 1984

Summer is an awkward season in Seattle. Short and intensely lived, routines get askew from the long days and everyone suddenly social. It feels as if the city takes a collective sigh of relief when the fall rains begin. They begin later and later it seems.

These poems came in two bursts during the unusually long summer of 2017. The first, in which smoke from fires in British Columbia created a type of oppressive no-weather. Neither sunny nor cloudy, not blue or gray, just hot and uncomfortable, for weeks on end. The air growing more and more unbreathable. The second, on a surprisingly hot morning in early September, when I woke to soot pelting me as I lay in front of a window fan and to find our entire house filled with forests from hundreds of miles away. *This is our future.* I understood then I'd been writing about fire all summer. And it was then I started thinking about forestry school again.

🌲

I didn't exactly fail Dendrology, but it did what it was meant to do — made me reconsider what I was doing in forestry school. Thirty years on, I can still picture the specimen room in its 60s woodland veneer and drawer after wide drawer of well-worn wood blocks, the silent remove of the green world pressed and dried. Not a professor, not a pal's name, just this one room and the afternoons trying to grasp the patterns and details.

How did I ever end up in forestry school with only the vaguest sense of what a true forest might be? A simplistic reading of *Walden*? A naive sense of stewardship? A romantic notion of mountain striding? Perhaps any of these I would have enthused on at eighteen. But looking back, I can see my youthful interest was not in the woods at all, but in the cabin. Not that I actively sought or even understood solitude. I didn't, but clearly, as a closeted gay teen, I knew the desire to be hidden.

I never worked fire lines, though my father, making ends meet, did. Rather, I had a college work-comp job that was completely suburban — park maintenance and giving parking warnings at a popular summer reservoir. Intentionally placed there by the college to give me the most realistic picture of what I would be doing after graduation, it was dull. And authoritarian. And nothing like I imagined my life kindly helping kind people in the forest would be like.

This job also put forty miles between me and my college, giving me better access to a small city with a gay bar and porno shops where I could at least visualize some unruly erotic future I did not, at the time, understand how to have. More importantly, there were a few bookstores where I could browse without bumping into anyone I would know and where I bought Armistead Maupin novels that, of course, pointed to a very different social and urban life than where forestry would take me.

I can't recall exactly how I changed my major, just one morning feeling incredibly relaxed when I decided I would be better off studying English.

If you are a writer, you may be more familiar with the MacDowell Colony rather than the composer, Edward MacDowell, whose summer retreat and farm it was. In his lifetime, MacDowell was the foremost American composer, though the modernist revolution that we associate with Stravinsky and Schoenberg would, within the decade after his death, make his music seem somewhat quaint and distant. It's rare to hear his music live today. Orchestras are more likely to perform Ives or Copeland, music that rings livelier in our busy ears.

But there is that romantic beauty of his — a lush world of Euro-American destiny, unquestioned, as the music just spools out. I asked the pianist and composer Aaron Otheim to consider MacDowell's parlor music, a form that has mostly disappeared, and to reimagine these sentimental (and, at times, racist and sexist) tunes into something that would reflect our own age of climate anxiety, an age of endless fire.

The score you see in the book is from *Woodland Sketches*, a set of ten songs, including his most popular, "To a Wild Rose." What you hear in Otheim's music is an attempt at playing these burned scores — recorded through multiple microphones placed throughout the studio, physical manipulations to the piano, and electronic alterations and layering in post-production. What you read in that section of the book are my own riffs on MacDowell's songs and my own attempt to place them into a diminishing environment, removing any stench of manifest destiny.

♠

This unraveling — of music, of language.
A derangement.

In the last few years, I find myself worrying nearly every day about some aspect of the climate catastrophe, a worry that I suppose could manifest into some form of true psychosis, given the almost ridiculous focus on my own single organism in the face of planet-wide ecological collapse. I was at a New Year's party and had cornered someone who recently graduated college with my concerns about ocean acidification, or Florida being underwater, or the Greenland peat fires — who knows what I may have been going on about that particular night — but she looked at me and simply said, "But of course, everything is only going to get worse."

When?

And how *exactly*?

Now we learn Antarctica is melting faster than we estimated. The oceans are holding more heat than we anticipated. The coral is dying faster than we thought it would. China won't take our recycling. São Paulo will run out of water. I recently asked my doctor about starting antidepressants.

Trees show their history in their rings. We can read them like books — the wet years, the droughts, the fires. We can read the glaciers, the lake bottoms, the basalt layers striated with dust. Around us, in everything, is a book of change. As I have been working on this project, I have been thinking how queers tend to language and thinking of our own heartwood — those contractions and expansions that are unique to each of us. If we could read it clearly, we might make some sense of those years of hiding, a drought, which affects most of us in some way.

In those last few months of forestry school, as my anxieties built, I experienced not quite a collapse, but a distance from myself as I neared whom I would go on to become. I started to experience disorienting moments where the landscape would collapse about me and wipe my mind clean. Unable to remember where I was going or where I had come from, I would stand on campus sidewalks and quads as the trees slanted in all directions, waiting for these lengthening moments to pass. I started missing class. It got to the point I found it difficult to drive to work, pulling over several times while I caught my breath and waited for my mind to reassemble the scene around me. It is the only time in my life I have experienced synesthesia. In my case, colors becoming attached to sound, sounds to colors. It is a song that I cannot recall. I was fortunate in having an astute dorm RA who, watching me withdraw, insisted that I sign up for a visit to the campus therapist.

I visited the therapist twice. I am assuming that the first session was to make sure I was not suicidal, though I could certainly be misremembering on which visit she gave me some kind of assessment — one of those long lists of repetitive questions, meant to trip you up, and, as I remember it something much like a test one might use to find your major. As I sat in the office, watching her score my results, she looked at me and said, "Well, you score on this as if you are *very* homosexual, but you aren't, are you?"

A contraction, where there should be an expansion.

🌲

I often think there is a seam in queer writing, particularly in the way we write about the landscape. A site angle and distancing that reflects our initial distrust of the body and its longings, not the things we learn ourselves which make our lyric and erotic poetry so compelling, but a fracture in actual corporeality and solidity of things we have somehow wronged by our being. The world itself there, a solid block rubbed smooth by others and completely baffling.

Drawer after drawer, labeled, categorized, carefully studied — never quite making sense. Being queer means working things out from the negation, "*You aren't, are you?*" and that may be the gift we bring into language if we are lucky enough to find our way into being ourselves.

I sometimes wonder what my life would have been like if I had stayed in forestry school. If I had an advisor that cajoled me to work a bit harder, if I wasn't overwhelmed and terrified by coming out, and if I could have known that plenty of the work I would do in my future would also be just as dull as that first and only park job. I wonder what it would have been like to actually have had a decent therapist, when I needed it most, rather than a threat and shaming. At the time, and perhaps even now, in the small rural towns where so much of the work of land management happens — the tiny staff offices that dot the West — I'd still likely be living hidden and whatever idealized way of being solitary imagined in my teen years would be nothing but a type of suffering. But perhaps, I would feel more connection to doing something concrete to slow climate change, perhaps I would be at least scientific in my anxieties about the mass extinction we're in, perhaps I would feel less panic. Well, that's all conjecture.

I do regret that now when I go for a hike I can name only the most common trees and a handful of shrubs. I keep buying field guides and keys, which get brought home and then get shelved, put into day bags, taken back out and then never opened, a dead weight.

I saw in the paper that the Chechen government is encouraging its citizens to kill their gay relatives. How one can be kidnapped, tortured, and held for unrecoverable sums, money no one has. I read how a journalist was sentenced to a year in prison for interviewing a homosexual on Egyptian TV. There was a picture of a hanging in Saudi Arabia, an entire group of gay men, a broken ring of secrets needed to stay alive.

I live in a "socialist hellhole," where, if I desired it, my biggest problem might be getting a reservation for brunch or the traffic to get there. But I watch the news and worry. There's a bashing. Then another. It's naive to think things will remain the same, that the climate catastrophe will somehow leave our liberal democracies, fragile as they are, intact. That here, on the edge of the continent, in our affluence, we'll just carry on, slowly forgetting certain produce and summers with blue skies. Perhaps, perhaps. But it seems as likely that, in the catastrophe, the retrenchment in fear, authoritarianism, and religion will bode badly, as it always has, for the queers. We'll be hidden with our secrets and struggling with our truths, our language, kept to ourselves, alone.

It is that fear that drives this book — its fracturing, its side glances. When I was younger, everything I wrote was homoerotic, *the most unlikely things*, always homoerotic, as if I were embodying in language and narratives my joy in finally being seen, at being in a community, of finding love and pleasure. This is not to say the intent was to be unseen or somehow un-queer in this book, but rather in both my own aging process and in the current political environment, my sense of queering work has shifted. I cannot say this book is devoid of hope, there is that fox, stealthy in a pasture, but, admittedly, this book turned darker and darker as it went on.

And now we are here.

NOTES

Pg. 11: "The forest in the drawer" includes suggestions by Bill Carty during one of his workshops.

Pg. 18: "Some Burning : 2017" contains news headlines from 2017, edited for interest, data scraped by globalincidentmap.com.

Pg. 26: Aaron Otheim's burnt and altered scores are based on Edward MacDowell's *Woodland Sketches* published in 1896 by P. L. Jung (New York) and republished by Arthur P. Schmidt Company (Boston) after 1899.

Pg. 31: "A Swift Willing Light." The burning of the tundra and thawing of the permafrost in the polar regions may accelerate climate change beyond any of our most aggressive climate models. An unusually large fire burned in Greenland in 2017.

Pg. 41: "Autumn Almost" riffs on John Clare's "Autumn." He wrote many poems on autumn. His starts, "I love the fitfull gusts that shakes…"

Pg. 65: "Often a Meadow" creates another pasture for the fox from Melinda Mueller's poem "Radium" in *Mary's Dust*.

Pg. 71: "little shingles, little/ shivs" echoes Sylvia Plath's, "little poppies/ little hell flames" from "Poppies in July," which was brought to my attention by Aaron Shurin.

Pg. 85: "the purple deer" is based on an account in the opening of Norman Maclean's *Young Men & Fire*, one of the finest books I know.

Pg. 91: The epigram, "*Who, in the dark, has cast the harbor-chain?*" is from the Louise Bogan poem, "Putting to Sea."

Woodland Sketches

Edward MacDowell

The ARTHUR P. SCHMIDT Co.

Boston   New York

AUDIO

To download a recording of the music by Aaron Otheim and of Knox Gardner reading from this book, please visit our website, www.entreriosbooks.com/audio. Select this title and enter the password:

FIREWALL

Recorded at Jack Straw Cultural Center
Seattle, Washington

August 10 & 14, 2018
January 3, 2019

Recording Engineer: Daniel Guenther

Additional audio manipulation by Aaron Otheim
at his home studio in Los Angeles, California.